SKATEBOARDS

WHEELS IN MOTION

Morgan Hughes

Rourke

Publishing LLC

Vero Beach, Florida 32964

www.rourkepublishing.com

PHOTO CREDITS: Cover, pp 15, 18 Elsa/Getty Images; title page, p 17 Stanley Chou/Getty Images; p 4 Adam Pretty/Getty Images; pp 7, 21 Pat McBeth; p 8 PJ Heller/Getty Images; p 10 Mike Simons/Getty Images; p 12 Jamie Squire/Getty Images; p 13 Tony Duffy

Title page: *Skateboarding is popular all over the world—a truly global sport.*

Editor: Frank Sloan

Cover design by Nicola Stratford

Library of Congress Cataloging-in-Publication Data

Hughes, Morgan, 1957-
 Skateboards / Morgan Hughes.
     v. cm. — (Wheels in motion)
Includes bibliographical references (p.) and index.
Contents: In the beginning — The parts — Streetstyle — Special parks
— The ollie and beyond — Extreme boarding — Falling down — Equipment and repairs.
 ISBN 1-58952-668-6 (hardcover)
 1. Skateboards—Juvenile literature. [1. Skateboards.] I. Title.
II. Series: Hughes, Morgan, 1957-   Wheels in motion.
 GV859.8.H83 2003
  796.22—dc21
                                                        2003004051

Printed in the USA

CG/CG

Table of Contents

In the Beginning

For more than 50 years, skateboarding has been one of the most popular outdoor activities among youngsters around the world. In California, where some people say it all began, skateboarding was once called "Sidewalk Surfing." This was because it looked like wave riding but was done on hard, dry ground.

Girls, like Hong Se Lin of Korea, are among the best boarders in the world.

The Parts

The board part of a skateboard is called the **deck**. It is usually between 7 and 9 inches (18 and 23 centimeters) wide and roughly 30 inches (76.2 cm) long. Underneath are the **trucks** and **hangers**, which hold the wheels. The wheels are made of **urethane**. This is a substance designed to grip the surface and allow the rider the best control.

Skateboards are made of durable materials, built to last.

Streetstyle

Skateboarding can be enjoyed almost anywhere, from a driveway to a school playground. Many boarders enjoy testing their skills in an uncontrolled setting. This is called "street," because of the use of objects such as curbs, stairs, and railings that exist as natural obstacles.

With a little imagination, a serious boarder can always find a place to roll.

Special Parks

The growing popularity of skateboarding—and especially **extreme** skateboarding—has led to the development of specially designed parks. These feature ramps, jumps, half-pipes, bowls, and other challenging obstacles. Here boarders can test their abilities and try new tricks. These parks can be found all across America.

In skateboarding, balance is the key to everything.

Tony Hawk, the greatest boarder ever, soared above his competitors.

Nothing beats the thrill of big air.

The Ollie and Beyond

The most basic trick is the Ollie. This is the way boarders get their machines into the air. It requires popping the heel of the board down, then quickly shifting weight to the front. Skaters use this to go from the street to the curb or to mount any raised obstacle. It is used constantly and with practice can quickly become second nature.

The Ollie is one of the fundamental skateboard maneuvers.

Extreme Boarding

There are many varieties of skateboarding, from slalom (racing around cones) to streetstyle to downhill and flatland freestyle. A fast growing art form is extreme, where the jumps are much higher. Many tricks (spins and somersaults, for example) are performed while the skater is suspended in midair high above the ground.

Even the most skilled boarders always wear protective gear.

Falling Down

Here's a riddle to remember: What's the hardest thing about learning to skateboard? Answer: the ground. Falling is a risk with any new activity, but with the right protective gear and the right attitude (a positive attitude), you can avoid injuries and quickly master the skills of balance and agility.

Good thing he was wearing his helmet!

Equipment and Repairs

Keeping your skateboard in tip-top shape is a key to success and fun. Experts suggest **rotating wheels** regularly. Also it's important to watch for cracks in the hardwood deck and to keep it clean. Wipe moisture off the wheel trucks to keep rust from forming. Then lightly oil them from time to time for best results.

Most bike cleaning materials can be used to keep your board up and rolling.

CHAIN LUBE

RITCHEY
BICYCLE COMPONENTS

Cleans and Lubes
in one step

Shake Well Before Using

PRO

4oz. Danger: Flammable, read warning.
Keep out of reach of Children.

FINISH
LINE
Premium

EcoTech 2
Cleaner
Degreaser

A Bio-Clean
Breakthrough

▶ Totally Solvent Free
▶ Outperforms Traditional Cleaners
▶ Non-irritating, No Fumes
▶ 100% Biodegradable & Nontoxic

strength or dilute with water

20 oz. • 600 ml

ORIGINAL
**WHITE
LIGHTNING**®

**Self-Cleaning™
Wax Lubricant**

▶ Patented dirt "shedding" formula
▶ Chain, derailleurs & gears stay
  clean, work better, last longer.

#1 SELLING LUBE IN USA!

4 fl. oz. • 120 ml • Flammable. Read cautions on back.

**WHITE
LIGHTNING**

**CLEAN
STREAK**
METAL-PREP

▶ Quickly dissolves
  grease, grime and

▶ Dries rapidly leaving
  no residue!

▶ Prepares surface
  lubricant and e
  metal adhesion!

Flammable. Keep Out of
12.5 fl. oz., 350 ml
Read precautions on

PEDRO'S

**SYN
LUBE
ROAD**

synthetic
Chain Lube

DANGER: HARMFUL O

Please
Recycle

PEDRO'S

**BIKE
LUST**

SILICONE POLISH

Superior shine and protection from water & UV ra
Residual film makes future cleaning easier.
Made from the finest ingredients.

Lustrant supérieur protégeant de l'eau et des UV.
Laisse un film protecteur facilitant le nettoyage.
Fabriqué à partir d'éléments de haute qualité.

Superior brillo y protección con el agua y los ray
ultravioleta.
Su capa residual facilita la limpieza en el futuro.
Fabricado con los más finos ingredientes.

DANGER: CAUTION - EYE IRRITANT
Read carefully other cautions of the rear panel.

250 mL. Made in USA

Safety Tips

As a beginner—and even once you've gained some skill—you should always wear a CPSC certified helmet. Other suggested safety equipment includes wrist and elbow guards and knee guards. These are all specially designed to help new riders avoid the kind of injuries that will keep them from enjoying their sport.

Glossary

deck (DEK) — the flat wood surface, or board, a skateboarder stands on

extreme (ecks TREEM) — beyond the normal, expected level; very intense

hangers (HANG uhrz) — hold the axle and are attached to the underside of the skateboard

rotating wheels (RO tat ing WHEELZ) — switching wheels front to back, and left to right

trucks (TRUKZ) — metal suspension systems with shock pads to absorb impact

urethane (YOUR uh thane) — a compound used in making traction-gripping wheels

Index

Further Reading

Bibbins, Neil. *Bikes, Scooters, Skates, and Boards*. Storey Books
     Publishing, 2002

Noll, Rhyn. *Skateboard Retrospective: A Collector's Guide*. Schiffer
     Publishing, 2000

Takeda, Pete. *Skateboard: Your Guide*. National Geographic, 2002

Werner, Doug and Steve Badillo. *Skateboarding: New Levels*. Tracks
     Publishing, 2002

Websites To Visit

skateboard.about.com/mbody.htm

www.exploratorium.edu/skateboarding

www.unitedskate.com/

About The Author

Morgan Hughes is the author of more than 50 books on hockey, track and field, bicycling, and many other subjects. He is also an avid cyclist and professional musician currently living with his family in Connecticut.